MENTAL EXERCISE FOR DOGS

A STEP-BY-STEP ILLUSTRATED TRAINING GUIDE TO STIMULATE YOUR DOG'S BRAIN AND BUILD A STRONGER BOND WITH FUN HOUSE GAMES AND BRAIN GAMES

TABLE OF CONTENTS

CHAPTER 4
SIMPLE MENTAL EXERCISES AT HOME AND AWAY FROM HOME

CHAPTER 7
WHY VARIETY IN A DOG'S EXERCISE ROUTINE IS IMPORTANT

CHAPTER 8
BONUS: FUN AND CHALLENGING EXERCISE PROGRAM FOR YOUR DOG

CONCLUSIONS

INTRODUCTION

MENTAL AND PHYSICAL STIMULATION, HOW TO COMBINE THEM TO HAVE A HEALTHY AND HAPPY DOG

Dogs are highly intelligent; they constantly use their brains and their noses. The lack of stimulation in a dog can lead to behavior problems and stress, but we can avoid it by following some tips and actions like the ones you will see in this book.

The activity cannot be missing to stimulate them physically and put their brains to work.

There are endless activities that you can do with your dog at home and in a group or in a park where they go out. While not all activities are for everyone, there are always some that your dog will enjoy. For example, let him search the house for food, change toys regularly, teach him basic or motor skills (agility) training, play music, or try buying smart toys.

All the workouts you do have to be positive. You have to promote positive training with rewards. Rewards can be candy, a favorite treat, or a toy. In this way, training is always carried out positively. Research shows that this is the longest-lasting form of learning.

For his mind to work actively, don't stop stimulating his sense of smell.

A dog's sense of smell is thousands of times better than ours. The so-called "nose work" has been successful in many countries in recent years, teaching dogs to differentiate between different scents, just as police teach their dogs to distinguish between drugs and bombs.

When a dog uses his nose for a certain task, it's a wonderful mental exercise.

Another great way to energize your dog is to tackle various problems that occur in everyday life. There are many games based on the same principle. Even during his daily walks, he can solve problems, such as sending him to look for his "lost" ball. You can also hide in the forest and wait for him to come to you.

It also works to control the body. Training balance, motor skills, and body control is another easy way to stimulate your dog, as long as you don't put him at unnecessary risk. For example, you can teach your dog to weave between your legs, crawl under logs in the woods, turn lights on and off on command, or find lost items.

You are only limited by your imagination when it comes to training your dog. In this book, you will learn from the basics to the advanced so that you two can do activities at home and outside, sports that you can practice, and how to teach them to your dog.

Throughout these pages, you will find information on how and why mentally train the dog with the different games available and tested. Also, before starting the exercises, you will learn to read his body language and know that he can read yours.

Knowing this, you will be able to connect with him so that he has a healthy relationship with you and the whole family.

After this, you will learn to do mental exercises at home with what you have and simple elements that you can use, then, in a more advanced way, you will learn to prepare different toys that activate your dog, with advice so that you can adapt them according to the type of dog, such as the sticker ball that will be created according to the size of your pet.

You'll also find a chapter dedicated to toys you can buy or use from the ones you've made by now for when he's left home alone, along with tips on how long is too long to leave him alone. We will talk about the exercises later, knowing why it is important that you vary them so that he does not get bored. As a bonus, you can use another series of exercises and toys with your dog.

Thank you for trusting us enough to purchase this book, I hope it meets what you are looking for, we would greatly appreciate it if you leave us a rating and comment.

CHAPTER 1

TIPS ON HOW AND WHY TO STIMULATE THE DOG'S BRAIN (TO AVOID HAVING AN AGITATED AND RESTLESS DOG)

Owning a dog and caring for him responsibly means more than just feeding and monitoring the health of your animals. While these are very important aspects of the education process, there are other important factors. For example, stimulating your dog's brain.

A lot of attention is often paid to a dog's physical development, which is important because the activities a sitter does with a pet account for about 90% of their daytime exercise. Physical activity is essential for them because, in addition to keeping them happy, it helps them burn energy. Otherwise, they will develop bad habits like compulsive behavior, destructive personality, etc. It is also a great method to avoid problems related to stress and anxiety.

A dog's mental health has a great relationship with his physical development. Stress-related behavior problems don't go away if you can't reduce anxiety levels that come from boredom. Therefore, stimulating your dog's brain is crucial. The best thing is that this can be done while also being a fun activity for you.

Cognitive stimulation is all about asking your dog questions that he has to think about and work on to get a reward, which you can do with brain games for dogs. Working with your furry, this type of exercise will provide many benefits for him, such as:

- You will have greater control over your pets. He will pay more attention to you, so he will not have problems like running away or not following orders.
- Stability and emotional health for both parties. Although you often don't think about it, your dog can also be affected by emotions, which can greatly affect his behavior.
- You avoid behavior problems. Many of the behavioral problems that your pet can suffer are emotional issues: stress, fear, etc. By strengthening your bond with your dog, you can help him/her overcome these conflicts or not.
- You make the right connections. Not having an emotional connection with your dog is just as bad as having a false one. This can lead to dependency issues like separation anxiety.

The bond with your pet goes beyond feeding, brushing, and walking them, we are talking about an emotional connection that builds trust between you. This will let you know how your dog will react at any given time and make him feel comfortable and trusting with you. One of the best ways to strengthen this bond is to have brain games for dogs.

Ways to Start Stimulating Your Dog's Brain

Keep in mind the following information:

Start With the Easiest Level

If you make it difficult for him from the beginning, your dog will become frustrated and not want to continue playing. In the beginning—if necessary—you can help him by showing him how the different dog puzzles work.

Don't Leave Your Dog Home Alone

That way, you'll only make him associate it with your absence, which will act as negative reinforcement. Exactly the opposite of what we are looking for.

Horizontal Play

It consists of leaving several pieces of chorizo on the house floor. You can put them in plain sight first and hide them at home when you have control over the game content.

Vertical Play

Once your dog has mastered the level game, you can start placing treats at different heights (chair top, tabletop, etc.).

Smell Game

The smell is your dog's most developed sense, but many times we don't let him train it. Through the olfactory game, you will enhance this sensation. You can prepare something as simple as hiding treats around the house and having your dog go looking for them.

Dogs are intelligent animals with great learning capacity, but this intelligence must be stimulated. Just like children, they will struggle to develop if their abilities are not developed. Therefore, your dog needs you to provide him with things that will challenge his mind, whether it be through exploration, play, or a challenge.

Here are some exercise tips you can do with your pet to stimulate his body and mind:

Sports

It's that easy. Connect your dog with some type of exercise that he enjoys, and in this way, you will be combining his brain and body. For example, you can take him with you if you go for a walk, jog, or play ball games with him. If you want something more elaborate, you can try exercise circuits for dogs, although these require training and your dog knowing how to follow some instructions. These circuits are great for your pet because, in addition to obeying commands, they also allow them to concentrate.

If you prefer other types of activities, you can play inside the house, on the patio, or in the living room; this will be ideal for giving the dog a change of environment since you continue to expose him to other types of smells and sensations, which is good for him.

Taking him to the lake or the beach is always a good option. Any type of activity is important because it will allow you to deepen and strengthen the bond between the two of you.

Design Toys

Something ingenious and cheap that you can do with your dog is to design interactive toys with things that you have at home. Now that you know what your pet likes, you can use this to create some kind of fun and challenging artifact for him.

For example, you can fill a box with treats and let him figure out how to get them out, or you can just go to the nearest pet store and buy some of these types of toys to keep your dog entertained for hours. Later I will explain how to create them yourself.

Training

You don't need to pay a trainer. Just by following some basic dog training tips, you can work with your dog on routines, coexistence, and some basic rules, such as answering when called by his name.

The education of the dog is fundamental since this will allow him to establish a character to dominate it. Also, this will prevent him from acting out of character and will make him trust you more.

In the end, remember that some of the basic elements for your dog to develop properly are love, companionship, and the time you dedicate to him.

CHAPTER 2

DOG BEHAVIORS AND HOW TO RECOGNIZE AND UNDERSTAND HIS VARIOUS MOODS

Through how the dog positions its body, it can be known if he is happy, scared, restless, or other emotions. Joy, alertness, inattention, fear, or anxiety are some of the signs that a dog can show through its behavior, depending on each situation. Therefore, it is necessary to understand his behavior to educate him properly.

In this chapter, you will learn the keys to reading canine body language to understand their different emotions and to be able to keep them healthy while promoting a healthy coexistence at home.

What the Dog Pose Says

In general, it is easy to understand your dog's emotions if you pay enough attention to each of his gestures.

Their confidence and security are usually shown with their tail and head held high in an upright posture. When he needs to interact with another dog or owner, he expresses himself with hip movements, making him go into the play phase.

These animals are usually happy by nature, and the way they express their happiness is also through wonder. When they need to play, they put their front legs forward and their hind legs flat on the ground.

They show respect for authority when rolling from side to side. It is also an effective method when they decide to flee from any danger. The raised back is used to protect themself from possible risks.

When they are overwhelmed with insecurity, they may become immobile. He becomes paralyzed when an animal doesn't like something and prefers to isolate himself and take refuge in solitude. Disorientation is synonymous with boredom and stress, which is why they often walk aimlessly and only calm down when they are outside, playing, or jumping.

You Can Train Him with Love

The promise of guaranteed education is born when you decide to adopt a dog. The most important thing is to do it appropriately. In many cases, dogs develop hostile and incorrect personalities. The error here is in the training strategy that you apply.

Anxiety, stress, sitting on the couch, aggression, disobedience, and the need to escape are some attitudes that a dog can show when he is not taught to love. This is the best training technique:

Games and prizes should prevail during their learning process. Only in this way can dogs learn good rules of education and achieve the purpose of self-control. Socializing with other dogs will help him become a calm animal.

And it has been shown that a dog's emotional balance depends on its owner's emotional stability. The objective is to guarantee a calm and pleasant environment in which the animal responds positively.

Here is why it is important to know how to read your pet's behavior:

- Their joy is expressed when—among other things—they wag their tail animatedly.
- They can raise their paw to claim attention.
- They become rigid, and the whole body tense when they are in a state of alert.

There Are Ways to Work Its Attitude

The success of a dog's self-control lies in the good education he receives. For this, rules must be established and taught under the reward technique. That said, instead of scolding or even mistreating him when he does something wrong, start his learning process by rewarding him to change his behavior and develop a positive attitude.

This phase is essential because the animal will not only behave decently but will also show positive emotions. Effective communication is guaranteed, and the owner will understand every signal the dog makes.

Some tips to keep your dog in better shape are the followings:

- Keep animals healthy to increase their sense of security and confidence.
- You must know how to express your message on a physical level. In other words, exercise self-control in the face of any negative behavior on the part of the dog.
- Use games as a training technique. Scolding your pet will never get you anywhere.

It turns out that these animals can read human emotions through body language. Their sensory perception allows them to respond according to the treatments they receive. They just like to send out calming signals, especially when they are being scolded, to pacify the owner's attitude.

These signs are:

- Yawning.
- Walking slowly when feeling intimidated or insecure.
- Frequent sniffing.
- Immobility.

Dogs have developed this ability to communicate through gestures. The key is to optimize your educational process and observe them to understand what they mean in a given situation and act accordingly.

Canine communication ranges from tail movements to gestures, expressions, and vocalizations. They will express their mood in different ways.

The movement of his tail says what he feels. When your furry friend is happy, his tail will usually flick or slightly but downward at a 45-degree angle. However, it all depends on the type of game.

If He Is Afraid

Suffice it to say that it is normal for canines to feel nervous or fearful in certain situations. However, many factors, such as traumatic experiences or little socialization with other people or dogs, can influence this behavior.

It is important to ensure a safe and quiet space that meets all his needs, especially when a dog arrives in a new home. This will give him a solid foundation and make him an emotionally stable and sociable animal.

The consequent panting, tremors, salivation, social withdrawal, crouching posture, tail tucked between the legs, and aggressive behaviors are often some of the fearful symptoms that these animals may express. Knowing this is key to starting the observation phase to recognize when your pet shows happy, aggressive, defensive, or submissive postures.

This attitude is often common in dogs that are confined or live in confined spaces. If you are trying to figure out the cause of his nervousness, know that he should ideally develop social habits through play until he learns to build confidence and security. A positive emotional response should be part of the quality of life you give him.

Learn to Recognize What He Feels

Non-verbal language is how dogs communicate with their owners and other dogs. Some signs to acknowledge their feelings are:

- Barking. This is their way of asking for attention or expressing any discomfort or concern.

- Immobile or raised tail: Expresses aggressiveness, nervousness, or excitement. He shows insecurity when the tail leans towards its stomach and joy when it moves quickly.
- Relaxed mouth. This is synonymous with calm.
- If they retract their lips, this shows how stressed they are.

Dominant postures are recognized when the animal's ears are upright or forward, eyes are open, staring, a fully rigid posture, and the coat is erect. Baring back teeth and ears are common signs of aggression.

A wagging tail indicates a friendly attitude, wide eyes, and a low bark. Play and fun run in the blood of canines, which is why they show their desire to play by bending down and constantly wagging their tail.

When they are not in the mood and do not want to attack, they prefer to show submission by showing themselves fully back with one paw closed and their eyes closed.

Canine Observation and Memory in Animal Intelligence

The canine skills have exceeded any kind of expectations. These animals have demonstrated the ability to read human emotions simply by reading their sign language. That is, they look closely and can easily detect sadness, joy, or anger.

Their empathy stems from the relationships they develop with negative and positive attitudes. That is why they choose to show signs of affection or calm when reading any human attitude. This is a way to show solidarity and support for the host. This is where their ability to recognize and remember faces, smells, and movements come from.

What's Behind the Howl

Many factors can cause howling in dogs. They use it as an alarm signal or warn of someone's presence and attention when they don't like something. It is a way of communicating with other dogs as well because when they hear a sound, it is almost impossible for them not to repeat it, it is part of their nature.

Another theory is that these animals often howl when they show anxiety or nervousness, especially when loneliness overwhelms them in the absence of their owners. Crying is also associated with resentment when separated from the owner, even for hours.

This is because these animals are naturally sociable, and being alone affects their mental state. For this reason, in some cases, dogs choose to behave destructively, moving constantly and howling to attract attention and express their dissent.

It can also happen if they have had previous traumatic experiences or a lack of education. In this case, the key is to develop playtime skills like toys, teethers, and bones so he can learn to manage his anxiety and get used to being alone when necessary.

If He Has Pain

Often, you can tell if an animal is behaving abnormally. That is, they can be seen vocalizing erratically, licking themselves extremely, losing their appetite, having difficulty moving, and most importantly, being downright aggressive.

When a problem occurs, it is important to detect it early. The success of a dog's health lies in his constant observation and quality care. Therefore, when an animal exhibits unusual behavior or is depressed, he should be evaluated immediately.

The most common symptoms of possible disease are:

- Apathy. Canines are normally active throughout the day, expressing their emotions for a living, and love to play. If apathy happens suddenly, it's a warning sign.
- No food. Loss of appetite is arguably the most immediate symptom when the dog's health deteriorates.
- Alteration in his rest.
- Immobility.

Regardless, the smartest course of action is to take him to a veterinary specialist for evaluation.

Interacting With the Pet Is the Best Way to Have Assertive Communication

The success of having a perfectly healthy dog depends on your care and knowledge. Interaction with an animal is very important as it allows you to discover what is bothering him and every message he sends. Knowing how to read their language is crucial to understanding their psychological states, such as desires, pleasures, annoyances, and disagreements.

Knowing everything about your dog will promote optimal training techniques, produce positive results, and ensure a good quality of life for the animal.

Recognizing their different vocalizations, facial expressions, movements, and body language is one step in communicating with complete confidence.

You Can Make Your Dog Very Happy

In short, the owner's attitude can also affect the animal's mood. Therefore, only tokens of love should be offered, as it will be a good strategy in their learning process and will cover all their needs. In this way, the animal will feel loved, comfortable, and happy where he is and expresses nothing but gratitude.

Regular walks, constant companionship, exercise and play, healthy eating, restful sleep, periodic medical evaluations, and permanent grooming are part of the right of these animals to live pleasantly.

In addition, the presence of these animals has psychological, sociological, and therapeutic effects on humans. There are many benefits, such as increasing the feeling of well-being, reducing the risk of cardiovascular diseases, stress, loneliness, and depression, promoting socialization, the feeling of security, and daily exercise that contributes to a better quality of life.

Signs That Your Dog Is Lacking Mental and Physical Stimulation

We know that both dogs and cats need physical activity, although for some pets, it is not their ideal plan, and they get lazy. Obviously, some breeds need more exercise than others. For example, a daily walk is enough exercise for a small dog, but on the contrary, some dogs need at least an hour of exercise a day.

When we realize that our pet needs exercise and his size allows it, we should not limit ourselves to daily walks but combine them with games, competitions, etc. They are probably tired of doing the same thing every day and want to change places and routines. Do you know how to detect if your dog needs more exercise?

Be aware of these signs:

Has Weight Problems

If your dog has recently gained weight and is having trouble doing the exercises he used to, like getting on the couch or going for a fast run, he will need to exercise to lose weight. Keep in mind that obesity is a dangerous disease for your furry pet, which can develop into diseases such as diabetes in the long run.

If your dog shows little or no interest in food, it could indicate his unhappiness. On the other hand, in some cases, unhappy dogs decide to eat more because it helps them feel better. Any change in appetite—whether increased or decreased—can be a clue to your pet's mood. Changes in eating habits can also lead to changes in weight, so if you notice your dog has lost or gained a few pounds, it could be a sign that he's sad or depressed. He may feel lonely and may need you to stimulate his brain.

Has Destructive Behaviors

Lack of exercise can generate anxiety in dogs, and anxiety can generate movement, exhausting them through inappropriate behaviors such as scratching furniture, tearing carpets, digging holes in the garden, scratching doors, etc. We are already talking about severely anxious dogs when destructive behavior occurs, so this is a resource for you to increase their levels of physical activity, both qualitatively and quantitatively.

Lacks Interest in His Toys

Just like with us, a loss of interest in normal activities can be a sign that the dog is not feeling well. If your dog is usually excited about his toys and hasn't been interested lately, he may not be in his best emotional state. It's common for them to have little desire to play from time to time, but if this continues for a long time, it might be worth investigating what's going on.

He Plays and Moves Abruptly

Just like when your dog plays rough or beastly, it's a clear sign that he needs to go a long way. This should be a wake-up call. We can see that he has too much energy stored in his body, which makes him lose control more than usual when playing.

Does Not Want to Play or Exercise

Toys aren't the only thing that can cause him to lose the will to act. He can be brooding if he's low on energy and doesn't seem to want to play with what you always do with him. Of course, not all dogs are naturally social and energetic, so it's important to be aware of any changes in their normal behavior.

Hides or Shrinks

The dog can hide in the house for shelter if the dog is upset. If there is no clear stimulus that leads him to behave like this—such as fireworks—your dog may be emotionally upset. You should also pay attention to body language as your dog may withdraw, trying to make himself smaller. This behavior can also be due to low mood.

When Walking He Gets Out of Control

Sometimes we think of a dog pulling on the leash on a walk because he doesn't understand or learn to use it comfortably, but it could also be that your dog has so much energy that he doesn't need to walk, but rather he needs to run somewhere where he can vent. If you let him run, you will see that when he is tired, the walk will become more relaxed and without the pull.

Has Trouble Sleeping

When your dog can't sleep through the night and starts wandering around the house or even seeking attention at those times of the night, it's a sure sign that he needs a change in his routine. It is logical that if he has not done any type of exercise throughout the day or at night, he will be frantic and want to move and do something different. You need to make him feel more tired during the day so that he can rest at night.

According to the American Kennel Club, dogs sleep more than humans, specifically, they sleep an average of 12 hours a day. However, if you look at your pet's sleeping habits and notice that he just wants to sleep, it could be a sign that he's not happy.

Insomnia, on the other hand, can also indicate the same thing.

That way, no matter how much sleep your pets get, they can feel bad if it's significantly more or less than normal. It's important to note that insomnia can also be caused by physical pain, so if your pet is having trouble sleeping, it's important to rule that out.

Barks a Lot

Another more common behavior observed by dogs that are bored and anxious due to lack of exercise is incessant barking and howling. We know that a dog's barking is normal and there is nothing to worry about, but if it barks excessively you need to check and relieve his stress.

Remember that sometimes investing more time in exercise can improve his health and attitude.

Licks or Bites Excessively

When dogs lick or chew their paws a lot, it may appear that they are trying to clean or scratch themselves, however, it may be that they are trying to calm themselves down because they feel sad. Most people don't realize it, but excessive licking (or biting) can be a way to calm the nerves. However, if your pet licks or chews excessively, it's important to rule out insect bites or skin conditions.

In the next chapter, I will show you how to educate your dog so that you create a relationship with him and integrate him into the family.

CHAPTER 3

HOW TO EDUCATE THE DOG TO CREATE A UNIQUE RELATIONSHIP WITH HIM IN SUCH A WAY THAT HE INTEGRATES WITH THE WHOLE FAMILY

It is a universal truth that dogs are humans' best friends; they also leave a mark on our souls, however, to connect with them, you have to do certain things.

This has even been confirmed by the results of several surveys, which concluded that dogs and humans develop a bond similar to the one between parents and young children.

We know from experience that when relationships are strong, it's hard to imagine life without each other.

But sometimes, due to lack of time or other reasons, people feel that the relationship between dogs and humans is getting colder and colder.

Feeding your pet, taking care of his health, taking daily walks, or snuggling with him while sitting on the sofa are important things to consider, however, if you want to strengthen the relationship with your dog, there are more things you can do for him:

Positive Education, Always

The education of the dog is the fundamental pillar for you to live in harmony with him. Actively train your dog without punishment, with love and rewards, and you will have a confident animal that fits in and feels good. It's something I told you before.

Teach him basic signals like "sit," "stand," or "stay," and gradually add other commands you can do together.

You will notice that you care about him by educating him, and your affective bond will strengthen. An educated dog knows how to behave and will prevent you from having to control him all the time.

Know Your Dog's Personality

If you want to strengthen the bond with your dog, you must know his temperament, character, and needs. If he is outgoing, he will like other dogs and humans. If he is a bit shy, we will gradually introduce him to potential friends.

Try to know everything he doesn't like and everything he likes to avoid offering him. Notice when he is in an active mood and asking for calm, time for activity, or rest.

Make Eye Contact

You probably have heard of oxytocin, also known as the love hormone. This substance is not only about the relationship between people but also about the relationship between animals.

It turns out that when we look at furry animals, their oxytocin levels rise. Oxytocin reduces negative emotions, such as anxiety or stress, and increases confidence and relaxation.

So, don't skimp on a friendly and affectionate look at your fur because, with this simple act, you will go a long way in strengthening the bond that unites you.

Go on an Excursion Together

When you plan a walk with your dog, it already has many positive aspects that strengthen your emotional bond.

Because there is nothing that dogs like more than to frolic in the mountains together with their human friends.

For your dog, running, sniffing, and exploring new sights and sounds with you is an experience they won't forget, and neither will you.

Be Aware of Reading the Dog's Body Language

Dogs are intelligent animals, capable of expressing everything they want or need with gestures and expressions.

Through their body language, they tell us if they are sad, happy, stressed, or how much they love us. They always go out of their way to let us know what they want. We already saw that before.

Observation is crucial to grasp the meaning of each gesture. If he sneezes, yawns, and licks his lips, he may be nervous. If he showed us his belly, it would tell us he trusts us.

It is enough that we study the meaning of their gestures so that they feel understood and the affection they express to us increases.

You Can Pet Him with Dedication

There's something that you always have on hand, and it goes without saying what it is about, is the opportunity to pet your dog to strengthen your relationship. Do it consciously, give him all the attention he deserves, and forget about the phone, television, or social media at those times.

Try to make your dog feel that you are there for him. Before you start petting him, call him by his name, look at him from time to time, and talk to him in an affectionate tone.

Do Mental Exercises Where He Works His Smell

Doing some smell exercises with your dog will strengthen your relationship since this is his most developed sense, and his brain is going to work a lot.

Because they are in control of the situation, dogs feel safe and satisfied with the challenge of searching and finding our hidden objects.

There are as many variations of these exercises as there are imaginations of those who propose them: at home, in the park, in the field; using sweets or pieces of food that we would put in boxes or hiding places.

Give Him Massages That Relax Him

If you have a dog who loves massages, don't deprive him of the opportunity to relax. Start with a gentle massage behind the ears, neck, and back... as you go, you will find his favorite spots and the amount of pressure he desires.

This is another of the many ways to strengthen your relationship, and your furry will thank you infinitely.

Be Attentive to Him When You Walk

Make the most of every moment you have with your dog and really be with him.

Daily walks can be precious time, especially if you put problems and distractions aside and foster your connection with loving looks and words.

Focus on your furry friend, synchronize your steps with him, and let him know through gestures and movements that you enjoy spending free time with him.

Enjoy Going Out Together

When the weather is good, what better idea than to plan a walk and have a bite to eat in a wild meadow? Once you associate the word picnic with the great outdoors, you'll see him wagging his tail in wild delight.

Don't forget the baskets with tablecloths, snacks, drinks, dog food, and knick-knacks. You will have a great time and can also start mental exercises in those places.

Use this day to strengthen your relationship, play with him, and comply with his demands. A good day in good company will be all your dog will need to associate with a pleasant feeling that will make him love you even more.

Do Sports

A healthy way to build muscle and strengthen your relationship with your dog is to go for a run together.

In this way, you will both benefit because running alone is different from running with a partner who motivates us when we falter.

When your dog gets used to running with you on the mountain, the beach, or the park, he will be the first in the starting line.

Eat Together

Luckily, there are more and more bars and restaurants where you can spend quality time with your dog. This is the perfect time for a delicious breakfast or a relaxing meal in the company of loyal friends.

The image of people sitting at the dining room table with their dogs lying peacefully at their feet is priceless. Your dog will feel more important if you share a place you love so much with him instead of staying home alone.

Be Calm

If you want your dog to trust you and feel safe in your presence, even in situations where he's up to some mischief, and you're about to throw a tantrum, you need to stay calm.

Dogs are highly sensitive and can quickly pick up on the emotions of the people they live with. Do not be angry with him, do not yell at him, take a deep breath and try to make him understand what is right and what is wrong.

Try to Travel Together

Have you ever thought that traveling with your dog can strengthen the bond? If you have tried it, you know it is worth taking on short, medium, or long trips.

If it is the first time, you want your pet to be a good travel companion, always willing to go wherever you want to explore new territories.

This way, you also avoid having to miss him by leaving him in a shelter or at the home of a family member or friend.

When You Buy Things, Let Him Choose His Toy

The dog's mood when he enters the toy store is special, the moment of happiness floods his face, and at the same time, he gives you a knowing look as if to say, "I want this."

Since our dogs are like children deep down, why deprive them of these magical moments?

Take him to a specialized pet store and let him choose the toy he likes best.

By associating a new toy with the pleasurable situation you create, your dog will somehow become more attached to you.

How to Strengthen the Bond with Our Dog?

To restore or strengthen the bond with our furry, which provides us with so much complicity and security, we have to get down to work, be constant and have the necessary time.

Words of love make dogs feel safe, loved, and happy, but most importantly through actions.

Remember, they fascinate us all the time: when we educate them, when we train them to obey us, when we offer them smelling exercises, or when we simply turn them into our companions for trail running.

- Spend quality time with your dog. Contrary to what many people think, in the time you spend with your dog, as in so many other things, quality matters much more than quantity. In any case, practicing activities with your dog is the first step to building a good relationship.
- Avoid conflict. Find alternatives to obsessive conflict situations, however common they may be. If your dog doesn't want to get in the car, doesn't want to get up from the sofa, or asks you for food at the table... think about it: for all these "problems," we can use the environment without any qualms about having conflicts with our dog.

- No penalty, there are other ways. The punishment initially worsens and ultimately destroys the relationship. Punishment can destroy a dog's trust in its owner, and trust is the first step in building the bond that will later form the backbone of a good relationship.
- Do everyday things with your dog. Now, in the summer, many dogs love the yard as much as we do, and they love to "gossip" about everything that happens around us. This is just one example, you can take your dog anywhere!
- Give your dog a sense of security. Don't cheat them, don't let them down... don't play with things that are important to them (toys, "prizes," food...) if you're not sure they understand you. Many dogs develop resource ownership issues due to bad experiences.
- Practice communicating. This suggestion goes hand in hand with the previous one. If you must take something from your dog, do not take it indifferently but in exchange for something of at least equal value. You'd be surprised how powerful communication can be when working with difficult dogs.
- Give a clear message, very clear. This means that the combination of our words (which we think is most important but isn't), tone of voice (which is most important), and body language (the dog's first source of information) must be consistent and easy to understand (when there is a threat). Praise and rewards don't mean much in the same situation, right?
- Tell him you love him. Dogs need social reinforcement to feel part of the family. Some ask for caresses, others ask for simple eyes... respect your dog, do what is natural, don't force it, go back to the original, and everything will be simple.

Now that you know how to communicate with your dog, let's start working on mental exercises at home and on the go.

CHAPTER 4

SIMPLE MENTAL EXERCISES AT HOME AND AWAY FROM HOME

Dogs with active minds are happier. Stimulating a dog's intelligence is also a way to prevent boredom and thus, avoid unwanted behaviors such as destroying the house, barking excessively, or becoming too dependent. Engaging your mind with challenging games is one way to do this. Here are several mind-stimulating family games: Hide and seek, catch me, one two three, "what do you smell?", birds by the window, five minutes of music for dogs, a new trick, box games, meet my new friend, catching a frisbee, and much more.

Just like people, many dogs need to hold their heads up. For this reason, walks and social relationships with other animals and people are essential to avoid boredom in dogs and prevent more or less serious behavior problems, in addition to keeping their minds active. Finding a way to stimulate your dog's brain can make him a happier animal. Playing with dogs is a great tool to exercise their intelligence. Below I will explain what it is and how to do it.

The Game of Hide and Seek With the Dog

A busy dog is a happy dog. Asking him to carry his backpack on walks (with his personal effects) or take a newspaper home are activities that exercise his brain.

Another fun option is to play hide-and-seek with him. Sprinkle wet food on an object and hide it in a park or at home. If you play hide-and-seek with your dog at home, it's a good idea to cover the toy with a T-shirt or other old clothing to avoid making a mess in the room.

The search path may contain boxes, containers, and other obstacles that the dog must jump over. Food items can be hidden in various places along the way, and when he finds them, he can be rewarded with pets and even homemade cookies.

How to Do It

I explained to you before how you can do it, but I will explain it to you step by step:

1. Show him a sweet when you are in the living room, for example, and then you need to hide the sweet.
2. Go to a room and hide the sweet and then let your pet go; let his nose help him find it.
3. You can go from simple to more advanced until he has a bit of a hard time finding it.

Catch Me If You Can

Dogs will love this exciting and fun canine game. The idea is that he sees something that interests him and pursues it; that he uses his brain by investigating what it is about.

How to Do It

1. Tie a rope at least a meter long to the end of a long stick. Attach a small stuffed toy to the end of the string; now, you have an inexpensive pet toy.
2. Hide behind a door or wall and grasp the stick in your hands while the toy lies on the ground where the dog can see it.
3. When the stuffed animal manages to get his attention (you can move the stick a bit to do this), he will try to reach it with his mouth. At this point, you can intensify the movement to prevent the animal from grabbing him. So it becomes a game of creative capture.

One, Two, Three

Motivating a dog to act differently is another fun game to stimulate his mind. Cues to change activities (from picking up a ball to running down the hall for his toy to getting a hug, among other things) can be preceded by an energetic and friendly "one, two, three," and this works in the brain. In the same way, activate the modify action.

How to Do It

1. For this, you have to learn to read your dog's body language; knowing this, when you see that he begins to get bored of doing something or has already lost interest, change the activity.

2. Before doing so, you say, "one, two, three," and you two start another game.
3. In this way, you educate him a little so that when you want to change the activity, say these words, and he will understand that you are going to do something new.

I Smell, I Smell, What Do You Smell?

Playing with the dog to differentiate smells helps to work his mind.

A dog has an extraordinary sense of smell, thousands of times stronger than ours, due to millions of olfactory receptors in its cold, wet nose. Exercising this ability is a fun and stimulating game for a dog's brain. New smells can be shown to the animal (preferably if the smell is strong, especially the first few times), but the animal is not used to it. Commercial air fresheners and fruits are good options to start with.

How to Do It

1. Allow your dog to smell new odors (smells that can cause allergies should be avoided) and hide.
2. Rewards or treats will comfort the dog while exercising his mind.
3. The new smells will trigger a big question in his mind trying to find out what it is about what you show him.

The Little Bird in the Window

Dogs—just like us—love novelty. The plan is for him to see something changing happening all the time and his brain, always in investigative mode, will want to see those beings there, moving and active.

How to Do It

1. If you live in a house with a patio or garden, you can place a bird feeder in front of the window, providing the dog with an interesting and changing landscape, changing as new birds arrive in search of food.
2. You can put birdseed in these feeders so that the birds come on their own.
3. Once the birdhouses are in place, your role in this game is gone. For the dog, it will be fun entertainment that will help him feel less alone.

Five Minutes of Music for the Dog

These sounds provide sensations to the dog and are a resource to calm anxious puppies who become distressed when left home alone. In the same way, hearing a wolf howl or listening to a wild whale in the ocean stimulates a dog's brain.

Internet helps to get some of these sounds for free. Look for specialized sites with some collection of different and interesting wild sounds: from birds in flight to barking farm animals or other similar animals. There is no doubt that it is a stimulating entertainment for dogs.

Learn New Tricks

Teaching a dog commands, such as sit, lie down, or roll over, is another way to keep his mind active. Some classes and professionals specialize in training dogs, but some home obedience techniques can also help develop your relationship skills. These training sessions force the dog to activate its brain.

How to Do It

1. Remember to teach him basic commands, such as sit, come when called, lie down, or shut up.
2. You can have a clicker (for dog training); this can help in learning and make it easier for the dog to follow the dynamics of the game, although it is not mandatory. Once he has learned to sit, the newly acquired pattern can be incorporated. Adding complexity is one way to stimulate the mind.
3. When you teach him tricks, try to have prizes so that he wins them or interests him, if you see that he gets bored, don't force him to continue; leave for another day.
4. If you're not at your best emotional moment, don't try to train; they feel your emotions as well.

The Box Game

This is an exciting game for him, especially when it rains and you need to keep him active at home to combat the cold. You allow him to hide, show him objects to chase, hide toys to look for, and learn patterns, such as going in and out of a particular space.

How to Do It

1. You can behave like another dog, you two go and hide together,

you ask him to come with you, and you stay in a hidden space. Three can participate there, for example, you hide with the dog, and your partner or a child looks for you, and when you get discovered, you can put emotion—screaming and rejoicing.

2. Soon the dog will understand what it is about. You can also add the fact that you put an object with some candy inside and that he does not see where you hide it.

Introduce Others

A dog is an animal that loves to explore and sniff its new friends and companions. A walk in the park with a friend at home is ideal for playing this quick game that activates your dog's mental abilities. Introduce him to your human companion, and let him sniff and explore. If he likes them, the dog may show his affection by wet licking their face or hands. Remember, this is a passionate display of affection—a special canine kiss that stimulates his brain.

Capture a Disk

Throwing a frisbee is an engaging and motivating game for dogs. Once you've learned to throw and chase dishes with your dog, you may want to perfect the technique or even enter a tournament.

How to Do It

1. To practice it, you should have already taught him to pick up what you throw at him, you can throw him a frisbee or even a plastic plate that you don't use at home, although pet stores sell silicone ones that are softer for his teeth.

2. The plan is to exercise the dog so that he has to jump to catch it; this makes his brain activate, and he works studying the trajectory of the toy and catching it.

A Fun Doggy Massage

After so much activity, it's time for a good, relaxing massage to positively exercise your dog's mind. Why not try canine massage? Patience and consideration of techniques such as finding a quiet space at home or applying gentle pressure to vulnerable areas such as the neck are the keys to stimulating an animal's brain with our hands. Massaging a dog's ears can be especially pleasurable.

How to Do It

1. Ask him to lie down, and then you start to caress and massage him, caressing but with a little more force, behind his ears, legs, and neck.
2. Make circular movements in all areas watching his body language, where he feels most comfortable, stay there, and if you notice that it bothers him, don't continue.

Cupcakes

This is a challenging game, and your dog should not try too hard to figure out how to solve it.

How to Do It

1. Buy a muffin pan, preferably one that has six spaces.

2. You must place a prize in each space and a ball on it.
3. Your dog has to figure out how to remove the ball to find the treat.
4. You can put it in spaces where he is thinking about how to decipher the enigma of finding that prize.

Magic

Surely you have seen this game in many places, especially at fairs, in some cases, it is a type of scam, but in this case, we are going to stimulate the dog.

1. It is about placing three containers, glasses, or containers and hiding the prize under one of them.
2. This is a game that will allow your dog to develop problem-solving skills.
3. Start playing with the traditional "where is it, where is it," and you change the position of each container, and at the end, you let the dog choose where it could be. For this, he has to know where you put him at the beginning so that he can follow it with his eyes.

A Game at the Door of the House

Surely our puppy is not used to being left alone for long periods, and when this happens, he becomes anxious or stressed. One way to avoid this is to play on your driveway.

How to Do It

1. The game involves opening the door and giving your pup commands like "back off" or "stay" while you're outside, then shutting the door several times in a row.
2. This will allow him to develop self-control.
3. Don't let him suffer long, but try to make the time it takes to open the door and see him again longer, you will see that little by little, he will mature mentally to learn this.

Silent Games

The idea is that with these exercises, words are not needed so the dog can learn; below is an example.

How to Do It

1. If your dog starts to go outside, a game that can increase his intelligence is to walk with him and then stop at a certain point, so he knows to stop without you having to verbalize it.
2. This simple exercise will also stimulate his mind.

Candy Carrier Toys

These toys stimulate your dog since he has to get what the toy has inside. Hide his favorite sweets!

How to Do It

1. This is similar to what I explained before about hiding the toy for the dog to find, or you can leave him the toy and let him figure out how to open it to get the trinket, that's what his mind will work with.

Cardboard Joint Filled with Sweets

Stop thinking about throwing away toilet paper tubes! Save them all for this easy toy for your furry.

How to Do It

You just need to poke a few holes in the body of the toy—say with a pen—put the candy in it, and fold the ends so that they are closed on both sides. Your dog will smell his favorite treats and will do anything to get them.

Three Containers Exercise

It's an exercise where you can add more complexity as you go along. I will explain how to do it.

How to Do It

1. Find three containers and hide a prize in one of them.

2. If this is your first time tricking your dog, use a strongly scented candy so he can find it more easily through his nose. Pierce the container so the smell escapes better.
3. As you get used to the game, you can make it progressively more difficult.
4. The idea is that he chooses one of the three containers to find the sweet that awaits him.

Hanging Plastic Bottle

This is like a kind of *piñata*, but for your dog.

How to Do It

1. Thread the bottle to place the treats. Hang it upside down at a height your dog can reach and encourage him to hit the bottle so it topples over and the treats fall out. Let's see how smart he is!

Toy Storage

I'm sure your dog has a basket of toys in your house, and if you're serious about training, you've probably taught him how to put them away.

How to Do It

1. You will be in charge of throwing the toys around the house, and at your signal, he has to pick them up and put them in the basket. Repeat several times.
2. With this brain game, not only will your dog get tired of car-

rying them to his basket, but you will also reinforce this very useful command for canine parents.

3. The idea is to place the toy in the snout after having them on the floor. While grabbing it, get his attention and tell him to come with you and make him drop the toy in his basket.
4. At first, he may ignore you and not understand you, but with patience, he will understand what you are talking about. It's something you can associate with a command, so he always stores the toys.

The School

What better opportunity than taking advantage of a rainy afternoon to teach your dog a new trick or command?

Although studies have shown that some breeds are more intelligent than others, that doesn't mean that your dog, regardless of its background, can't learn.

It has been seen that a dog can learn up to 100 words, and they are even capable of learning gestures and signals.

You can teach your dog that all he needs is time and patience with active training.

How to Do It

1. Train your dog exclusively when you two walk.
2. Remember, sessions must be 15 minutes long. Keep your dog from getting bored and frustrated as much as possible.
3. After that, the session ends with a game of fetching a ball, tossing his favorite toy, or even a cuddle session.

Play with Obstacles

The idea is that your dog tries to overcome these obstacles and does it with great ease, in each game, you can change their position.

How to Do It

1. Install an agility barrier in your hallway that your dog can safely jump over.
2. You can use a broom, chair, bucket, etc., and invite your dog to overcome the obstacles with a treat in hand.
3. Not only will you be irritating his nose, but you'll be working out by burning off the kind of energy you can't while walking down the street in the rain.

CHAPTER 5

ADVANCED MENTAL EXERCISES AT HOME AND AWAY FROM HOME

Today we have many toys for dogs: chews, food dispensers, puzzles... each one of them is designed to fulfill a function more than pure entertainment, such as promoting smell, relieving the pain of a puppy's teething, or stimulating his mind. With all this in mind, in this chapter of advanced exercises, I will teach you how to make some toys with things you have around the house.

Homemade Kong

If you don't have a plastic bottle, don't worry! You can make a smaller toy food dispenser out of cardboard toilet paper rolls. This version is great for toy dogs, dwarfs, or small dogs and puppies, but not for big dogs or dogs that play rough, as they will most likely end up tearing it and, in the worst case, eating the cardboard thing.

These cardboard rolls give you a variety of possibilities, but we're going to highlight two easy ways to make candy-filled toys.

How to Do It

1. Just like in the previous chapter, you can flatten the corners or make a lid on it and open holes or seal it as you wish.
2. The plan is to get him interested in investigating what's inside.

Cardboard Ball

A ball is another way to stimulate him.

How to Do It

Take a roll of cardboard and some scissors, and follow these steps:

1. Cut 5 rings.

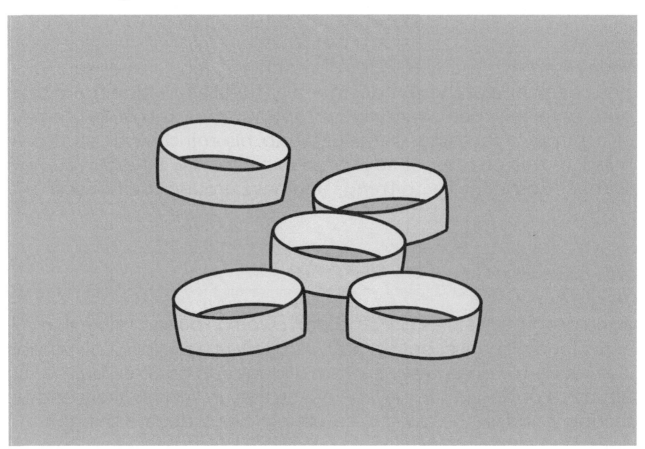

2. Insert the rings one by one into the other to form a ball with a small hole.

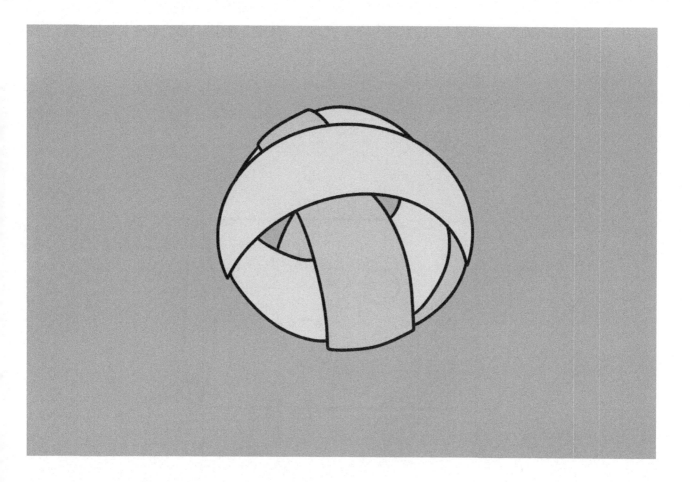

3. Through the holes, put treats and let your dog try to get them out by moving the ball.

Kong Tube

For this one, in addition to the cardboard roll, you will need a cutter to drill the holes. If you don't have one, you can use a knife or scissors, but be very careful. These are the steps to follow:

1. Use a cutter to poke holes in the entire roll, except for the ends, since you have to fold them. Remember that the size of the

hole cannot be too small or your dog will not be able to re-move the treat.

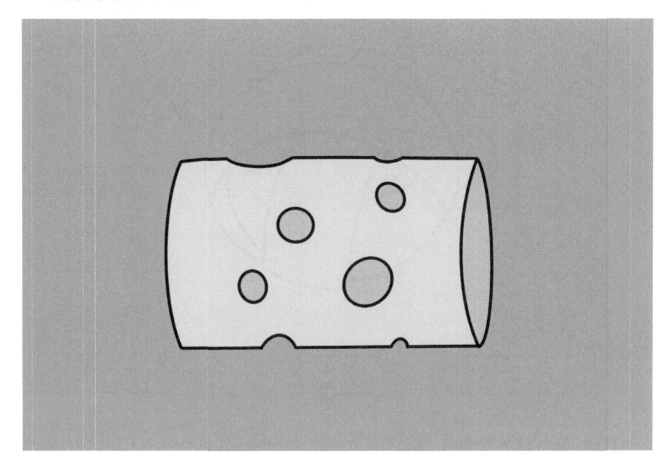

2. Close the roll on one side and fold the ends under.

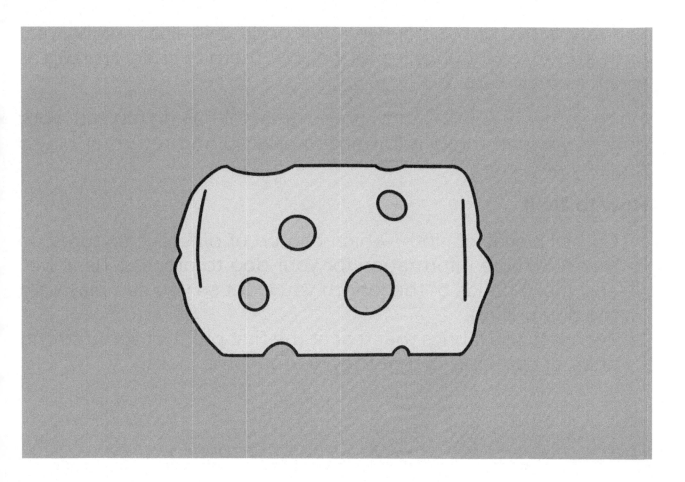

3. Insert the candy and close the other side.

Both toys are considered mind toys because they also stimulate the dog's mind by motivating him to try to get the food. However, remember that it is important that your dog doesn't eat card-board.

Homemade Teether Made with T-Shirts

Do you know the typical rope teether? You can make them at home with old t-shirts! Instead of throwing them away, give your dog a new lease on life by making this simple homemade toy.

For very active or hyperactive adult dogs, it is also a highly recommended toy for puppies, as it allows them to chew and tug as much as they want.

On the other hand, this chew is also great for having fun with your dog, as you can throw it for him to pick up and return or play a tug-of-war game.

How to Do It

1. Gather pieces of cloth, which can be of different textures, so that it is more information for your dog to process. Tie it well and make braids of the length you want so you can play with the dog pulling.
2. Try not to use fabrics that tear at the first pull, but some strong ones, or combine so that they do not come loose.

Homemade Teether with Socks

If you don't have an old t-shirt, you can also make dog toys out of socks! You can use any type of old socks that you no longer need, but it's best to avoid socks made of wool, as your dog is more likely to tear them and swallow the fabric.

With two socks, you can make a simple chew for a less destructive puppy or dog, since it's a cloth toy, more destructive dogs are more likely to end up tearing it. Anyway, we will also give you some tips to reinforce your toys.

How to Do It

1. Take a sock and cut the closed end to make two slits.
2. Fold the other sock into a ball and insert it into the previous sock, placing it in the center as a ball.

3. Tie a knot at each end, so the ball is fully connected and secure in the center.
4. If your dog is not very destructive or reinforcing, you can leave them as they are. To do this, cut them into three or six strips.
5. Make one or two very tight braids from the strips you cut, then tie them back together at the ends. This will make it more difficult for your dog to break the end of the toy.

If your dog is a puppy or an adult who loves to play, you can make a simpler toy:

1. Take a sock and tie different knots, keeping them as close together as possible.
2. If your dog likes to play with the strips without tearing them, you can leave the ends blank so you can cut them into different strips.

Both toys are great chew toys around the house, but they are also great for you to toss and encourage the dog to pick up and fetch.

Homemade Intelligence Game with Cans or Bottles

While we have seen several homemade dog toys considered homemade, I am going to show you a more difficult toy that is perfect for you and your dog. This way, you build the toy step by step so that you can learn and develop together.

The toy consists of a container for the sweets, supported by a wooden stick (it can also be plastic made), and your dog can turn the container so that the sweets fall out. Depending on the size of your dog, you have to adjust the size of the toy. Thus, for small or medium-sized dogs, a 33 ml can or vial will suffice, on the other hand, for larger dogs, you will have to use a larger container. The same goes for the sticks that create the structure.

To make this toy, as I just told you, you can use empty cans or plastic bottles, so it's great that these containers are reusable. Also, you will need the following:

- Pieces of wood or plastic that you no longer use and want to reuse
- Some sheets of cardboard (you can cut out cardboard boxes that you no longer use) or a wooden base
- Silicone or animal-friendly glue
- Knife or scissors

Once you have all the materials, follow the next instructions:

1. First, you must create the structure that holds the food dispensing container. To do this, you can glue different cardboard as a base in case your dog is small or medium. Once glued, you can cover them with masking tape to complete the mounting base. If you have a large or strong dog, we recommend choosing a wooden base or something more durable than cardboard. The size of the base depends on how many containers you are adding.

2. If you are using a cardboard base, you can use two sticks or even a pencil. In either case, you will need to staple them to the cardboard, one at each end, and secure them with silicone or glue. If you have used wood, use sticks or strips that are equally strong, and use silicone or glue that is strong enough to prevent them from coming off easily. You should now have a base with a vertical rod.

3. Take the container you will use and make two vertical holes so that the sticks that hold it to the previous structure can go through them. Insert the stick and check that the container rotates smoothly. If not, make the hole bigger.

4. Fix the pole with the container at the end of the structure. You can use silicone or glue again. Again, you can secure it with tape.

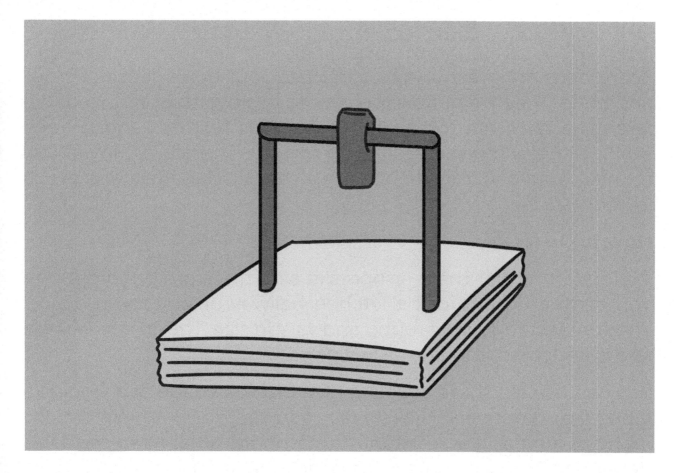

5. Before letting your dog play with his new toy, let it dry completely.
6. Let the dog explore treats or treats inside for his brain to work.

If you are a person with knowledge of DIY, you can use screws to assemble the structure of the toy, which will make it much more secure.

Your dog may not understand this game at first, so teach him that if he turns the bowl with his paw or nose, the food will fall out. Gradually you will realize that he understands and likes this toy.

Homemade Olfactory Mat

Scent pads are great toys to stimulate your dog's sense of smell and brain. They are quite expensive toys, since they consist of different parts within the mat, with various textures and shapes, making the game more or less complex. Therefore, I invite you to make your own rugs to achieve a very similar effect at a much lower cost!

How to Do It

Perforated rubber mats or non-slip sink mats are good options. You can find them in the kitchen hallway or buy them online. They are rectangular or round and vary in size. The 30 cm x 40 cm size is perfect for medium-sized dogs.

You can use old shirts or socks. Or a blanket made of a wool-like fabric that is not very thick. In fact, you can do it with almost any fabric as long as it is resistant. The amount of fabric needed will depend on the size of the rubber mat you are using.

Here are the steps:

1. Cut fabric, t-shirt, socks, blankets, or a mixture thereof into strips 3-4 cm wide and 15-18 cm long. Don't push too hard: You don't need to be very precise, and the irregular strips also allow for a more spatial variety for the toys. Of course, you will need a lot, and although the exact number depends on the size of your carpet, calculate between 250 and 300 strips.
2. Knot the end of the rug first: Thread the strip through one hole and out the next; to secure them, tie an overhand knot. Repeat to advance the other strips lengthwise. The next row is knitted vertically, passing the strip through one hole and out the hole below.

3. And so on: knit each row in one direction (one lengthwise and one vertically) until all the holes are completed.
4. Start small and keep it simple. At first, a few balls of food scattered on the floor around the toy will suffice. And give him a guideline like "find them" so he knows the game is on. When your furry friend is done eating them, sprinkle another handful on the carpet so he can see you.
5. And repeat the phrase, "find them!" The dog will understand! To make things even more complicated, in later stages, hide the kibble better and better between the strips inside the mat. Contrary to what happens with other food puzzles, you should never leave your dog alone on the carpet. You must always supervise the game because your friends can tear the strips and swallow them.

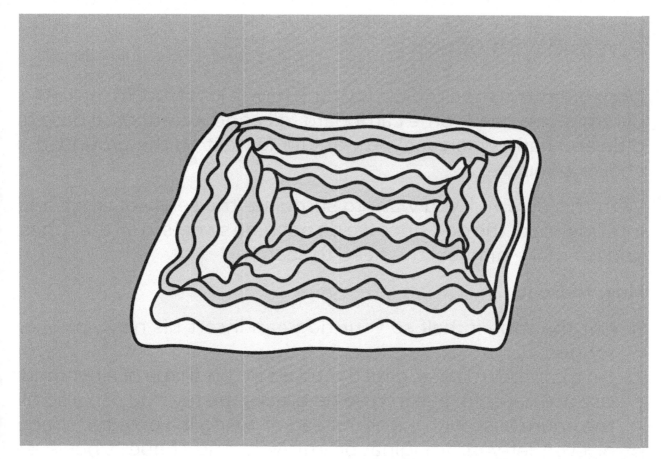

Homemade Stuffed Animal for Dogs

If your dog likes stuffed animals to play or sleep with, and if you like to sew, making them at home is a great idea. Also, especially if your dog tears them up a lot, it's much cheaper to buy enough fabric and stuffing to make a couple of stuffed animals, so you'll save a lot of money.

In this case, the way to do it is with your creativity, you only need padding and old fabric, a little creativity, and nothing else. Take care not to leave pieces that can be swallowed, such as metal buttons or pieces that can be swallowed by biting.

Pyramid with Candies

Dogs often love the simplest toys and have a lot of fun. To make this pyramid, you need some cardboard rolls, and a cardboard base to glue and hang wherever you want (or leave it on the ground; the choice is yours!)

With this pyramid, you want to stimulate the sense of smell and intelligence of the dog since we do not hide sweets in all the tubes, and we make him feel the need to search.

How to Do It

1. Cut the tube in half so your dog can insert his nose, paw, or tongue.
2. On a cardboard base, glue the tubes in the shape of a pyramid. Use animal-safe glue in case he breaks the toy. You can also fill the entire base with tubes instead of giving it a pyramid shape or even let your imagination run wild and shape it however you want. These shapes can make the game difficult.

3. Let it dry completely, and insert random candies into a few tubes.
4. If you want to hang the toy on the wall so your dog doesn't have to hunch over it, especially an older one, you can attach a piece of string with silicone or glue.

Box with Paper Balls and Prizes

This is a brain game that you can play with your dog.

How to Do It

1. In a box, put little paper balls (in which you will put the prizes) and also throw other loose prizes into the box.
2. You can make it more difficult: Put some paper balls without a prize, close the box, and put something in the middle that they have to push to get the prize.
3. You can also make it easier: Do not pack the balls too tightly and make it easier for them to find the prize quickly.
4. The shallower the box, the easier it will be for them to dare to stick their heads out and go around and around to get the prize.
5. Remember to adjust the difficulty level of your dog so that he can tackle the game.

Bottle with Prizes Inside

This is another idea for you to stimulate your dog mentally.

How to Do It

1. With an empty bottle or can, he will find things easier, give

him some treats, and the dog has to figure out how to get the treats out.

2. Another option is to poke holes in the can/bottle so that the prize comes out when pushed. The more holes you put in place, the easier the game will be for him; remember, the hole should be bigger than the size of the prize inside.

Snake with a Prize Inside

This is a toy that you can fill to entertain and stimulate your dog, and here are some guidelines to get you started:

If your dog is wary of novel stimuli, then you must be careful about presenting him with toys that you want him to associate positively with.

How to Do It

1. You can make the snake with the material you want, and that lets you be confident that it will not be eaten; it can be rags, long socks, or whatever you have at home, use your imagination.

2. In principle, you can leave the snake on the ground, let the dog explore at its own pace, and wait for it to adapt to the new elements.

3. If you want to use it as a food dispenser, start with the easiest steps, put some dry food in it and make sure it is smaller than the opening of the snake so it can fall out easily. As the food drops during play, you will encourage more play, add more dry food, and resize so the dog begins to learn how to manipulate the toy for larger pieces of food.

4. In the next step, to add one more element to the toy, you can put dry food inside it and then put some pate or wet food on

top. The addition of wet food adds to the licking element of the toy.

5. Many dogs will spend a lot of time licking and chewing on snakes before continuing to play and pick up other treats, making this toy a great addition to an environmental enrichment program.

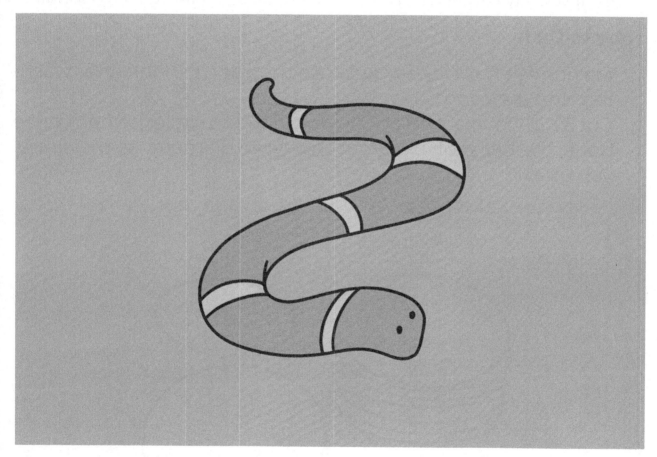

Important note: If the dog finds it difficult to get food from the snake, even following the tips above, the tip of the tail can be cut off to allow the food to flow through the slot. Remember, he'll get frustrated and lose interest if he doesn't get his food.

Make Your Own Sniff Ball

This ball is a suitable game for dogs with some experience with these toys since food remains are not easy to remove. It is recommended to start with larger chunks that are easier to achieve and then gradually make them more difficult by making them smaller.

How to Do It

1. Making felt balls is easy because they don't shrink after washing, and they don't fray.
2. Cut 32 20-cm diameter circles (or 24 16-cm circles), when you're done, the balls will be about the same diameter as the circles you used.

3. Fold the circle in half and punch a hole at the tip (then there are 4 holes in the circle). Use an awl, paper hole saw, or scissors.

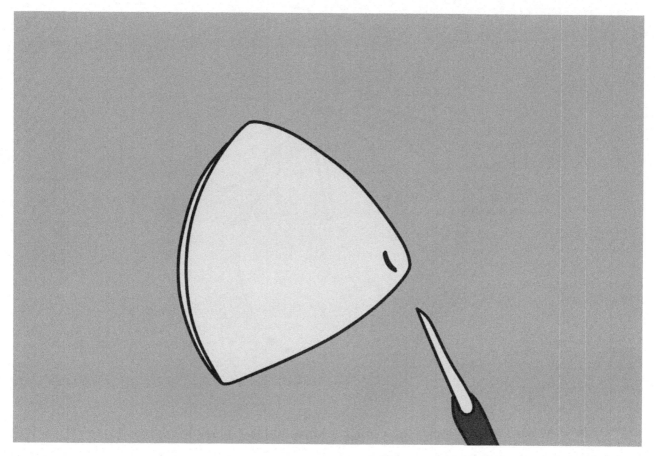

4. Take 4 zip ties and put 8 circles (or 6) on each zip tie.

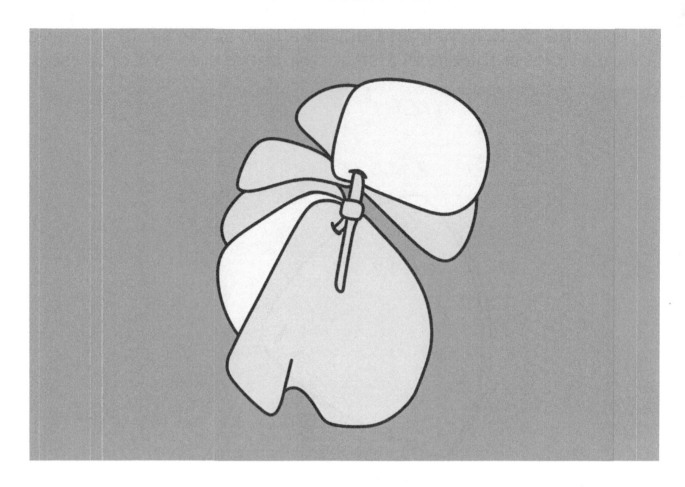

5. Close the flange and connect the other three on different sides to the first one we closed.

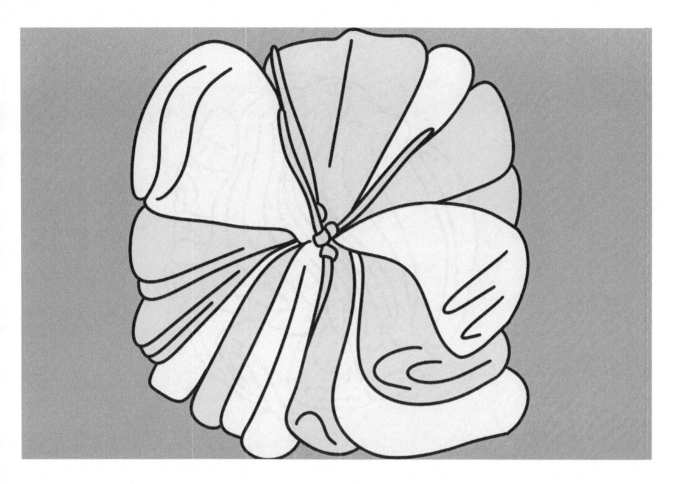

6. Then close the flange well and cut the end.
7. To prevent the finish from being too sharp or scratched, use a bit of sandpaper. It can also be melted.
8. A 20-cm circle forms a 20-cm diameter ball. So you can adjust the size of the ball by cutting bigger or smaller circles.

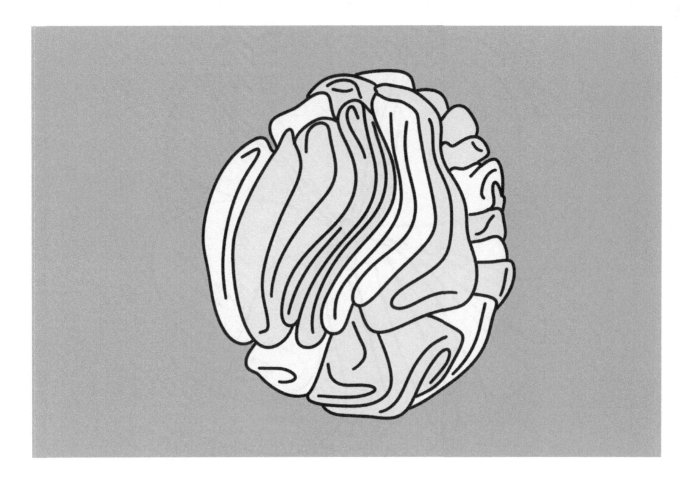

Box with Leaves and Between the Leaves Prizes

Another mind game you can play with your dog is using leaves.

A box where you put leaves and you throw prizes/food.

Guaranteed fun! You can put it in the background and he pokes around looking for it.

Towel, Blanket, or Stretched Blanket with Prizes

Another idea of games at home to mentally stimulate dogs is this:

How to Do It

1. Stretch a towel/rag/blanket, place some sweets/food on it, and roll it up. This will be the easiest step. He has to touch the roll with his nose or paw to open it, once he understands how it is, you can tie it to make it more complicated.
2. The plan is for the dog to start unwinding, looking for what's inside.

Ball Made with Fabrics or Ropes and Prizes Inside

With this game, I will show you another way to mentally exhaust and delight your dog.

How to Do It

1. In this case, it is a ball where you will put a cloth/rope with a prize, and the dog has to try to get the cloth and then the prize. You can also put other things that interest him.
2. Always remember to go according to your dog's level; it will cost him a bit, but he can do it little by little while he learns.

Sticker Ball

This is an interesting game, but it requires you to be careful.

How to Do It

1. If you have some stickers saved—like the ones that appear in

a notebook—try to make a large ball (about the size of a tennis ball) as compact as possible. Once you've done that, watch your little pet drag it around the house.

2. This option is great for small dogs, as larger dogs will destroy it in seconds. Also, it is not good for your dog to ingest the glue from the stickers. So you need to make a ball that is big enough that it won't fit in his mouth. Another option could be to cover it with a thin cloth or fleece.

Plastic Tube Covered with Fabric

This one looks a bit like the ones we've done before and has the same goal; let's see the steps:

How to Do It

1. Use a long tube, fill it with granules, and cover it with a cloth or thick sock.
2. Be sure to sew the edges well so that the ball does not slip out and roll, and you will immediately see your dog start playing with it.

Surprise Ice

This is a delicious game and also entertainment with the dog for a while, although it is not very hygienic.

How to Do It

1. If your dog doesn't bother water or cold things, and you don't

mind cleaning up the mess afterward, you can freeze the broth with beef or chicken cubes.

2. Many dogs love to play with ice cubes, and it's even better if it tastes like their favorite treat.

Patchwork Rope

Patchworks are always an option for you to entertain your pet:

How to Do It

1. If you have a lot of clothes at home that no longer fit you, you can use them to make a long rope to use as a toy for your dog. All you have to do is tie each garment one by one. Lastly, try to make a kind of little ball, as this is the part that your dog will hold in his mouth.
2. This toy is made to be thrown like a ball, you just have to spin it like an arc for your pet to carry it. It can also be used as a pull, but the knot may not hold as long due to the way you tied it.

Surprise Eggs Basket

Don't throw away the eggs basket anymore, now you can use it this way:

How to Do It

1. Egg cartons from the supermarket make great makeshift dog toys.
2. To use it, all you have to do is hide the prize or some of its goodies in the holes of the box. Then close it and cut a few small

holes so your dog can smell the scent. Pass it on, and you will see how he spends a few minutes admiring his discovery of how to open it.

Clothing Bone

A bone can be a toy that he plays with and his mind focuses on chewing on it.

How to Do It

1. Using clothes you no longer wear, draw and cut out a pattern in the shape of a large bone.
2. Once you've cut the design at least twice, sew the ends together and tuck them in with strips of clothing until smooth.
3. In the end, you'll end up with a premium chew bone that your pet will love because it even has a bit of your scent on it.

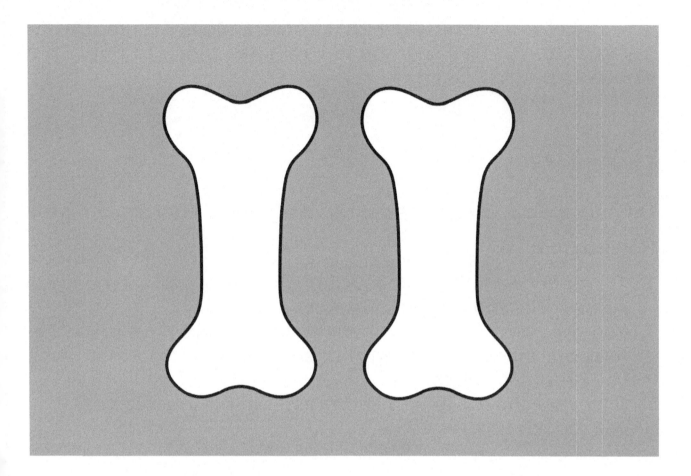

Towel Maze

It doesn't take a lot of materials to make fun toys for your pet. A single towel is enough to create a kind of maze where he can get all the treats with his nose and paws.

How to Do It

1. All you need to do is spread out a towel and put some treats or food on it. Then, place your hand in the center and rotate it as if you were doing a whirlpool.
2. The result is a scroll that hides a variety of treats. Encourage

your pet to lead the way with his nose and paws. Sure, it won't last long, but he'll spend a few minutes trying to figure out how to unroll it.

Squeaker Toys

Do you have a pup who loves things that squeak? Consider this toy.

How to Do It

1. Try putting together this easy DIY squeaky toy. All you need are some socks and old toy squeakers, and voila!
2. You will assemble a doll similar to the one we have made before, but place something that squeaks inside so that when you press it, it will sound.
3. Then you show it to him and press it in front of his nose, you will see how interested he is.

Puzzle with a Tennis Ball

Are you looking for a really easy way to entertain your dog? You can make a tennis ball puzzle. Dog puzzles are a great way to give him some extra mental stimulation. Best of all, this puzzle is very easy to do.

How to Do It

All you need to do is put some goodies in a muffin tin and place tennis balls on top to hide them. There you have it: you have your very own homemade dog puzzle. The plan is for him to look in which of the holes is the candy.

Interactive Tennis Ball

This is another of the simple toys that you can make with an old toy at home.

How to Do It

1. You're just going to open up a tennis ball and fill it with treats and voila.
2. You can show it to him so he can find out how to open it, or you can hide it.

Teach Your Dog the Names of His Toys

Some dogs can learn up to 100 words and can choose any of the many toys by name alone. Not all of us can be so successful, but he can learn a few, at least the ones you have at home.

How to Do It

1. Begin by playing with a specific toy, naming it as he goes.
2. After some practice and praise, your dog will assign that name to the chosen toy.
3. Once your dog has learned the name of that particular toy, you can test his skills to see if he can distinguish it from his other toys.
4. Then you add another one, when you show it to him, put the rabbit in front of him, for example, and say "Rabbit" or "George" or whatever name you have given to it, and so when he learns, you tell him "Bring Rabbit" or "Rabbit" and he will go to look for it.

CHAPTER 6

GAMES FOR WHEN THE DOG IS LEFT ALONE AT HOME

Leaving your dog alone at home is a situation that we cannot always avoid. Usually, a few hours a day is harmless to a dog, however, sometimes a pet's loneliness can wreak havoc if not handled properly.

Take into account these toys that you can buy from the many brands that handle them or you can make them, several of them we already discussed in the two previous chapters.

Interactive Toys

Interactive toys with sounds or lights are excellent companions for the dog that must be left alone for a while.

The sounds in many of these toys stimulate dogs' natural hunting instincts and encourage them to continue playing.

Any dog would love to play with a toy like this. It can be one like the one that squeaks that we did before or one with lights that he will surely love.

Food Dispenser Toys

Bars are the most common choice when it comes to food distribution toys. It is a rubber ball with a hole inside. Its main function is to fill it with dog food.

When the dog bites them, the candy is taken out, so while energy is spent, it is also rewarded.

This quality makes these toys ideal for dogs with little appetite. If your dog thinks food is part of the game, it will take it without a problem.

The same function works for dogs with the exact opposite problem. Dogs that really want to eat can accidentally choke, so this dispenser toy is ideal for controlling your dog's excess appetite.

These types of toys are durable, so you can allow your dog to chew on them with peace of mind without worrying that they will break into pieces and choke your dog.

The gong material makes this toy bounce unevenly, surprising dogs and making them love it even more.

Intelligence Toys

Intellectual toys are designed to stimulate the intelligence of dogs. There are different levels so that your dog learns to use them little by little. Start with the easiest levels and gradually increase the difficulty as the dog adjusts to the challenge.

The idea of these toys is for the dog to follow a series of steps to get a prize hidden in the different openings.

You must teach your dog to play with these types of objects. If he doesn't know how it works and doesn't get the results he wants, the dog will become frustrated, and you will have the opposite effect of the problem you originally intended to solve.

Stuffed Toys

The stuffed toys are the perfect companions for calm dogs and puppies when they are home alone.

In the case of puppies, it also helps to prevent them from crying at night since they often have separation anxiety problems, even when you are in another room. Remember, a good stuffed animal can greatly help your dog with anxiety.

Stuffed animals or plush toys are perfect for puppies to chew on, as they satisfy their urge to chew while massaging their gums and allowing their teeth to develop properly.

Choose stuffed animals with strong seams or with a double cover, this will make these types of toys last longer. Or you can make them yourself just like I taught you before.

Rope Chew Toys

Rope toys are ideal for your dog to chew on when bored. In addition, this toy's shape helps maintain proper oral hygiene for your dog, as it removes tartar and food debris.

You should check the condition of the rope regularly. When you notice that they begin to wear out, you should throw them away and replace them with another that is not defective.

Scent Mats

Scent mats or blankets are toys specifically designed to stimulate a dog's sense of smell and encourage him to get into the fetch game.

It is a fabric with other components arranged in different ways. The goal is for the dogs to use their noses to find different treats hidden in the folds of the carpet.

As a tip, you can mix several types of dog treats. This means more variety of scents and, therefore, more fun. You can use it like the ones I taught you before.

Make Your Own Canine Circuit

If your home allows it, you can build your dog his own obstacle course. The level of complexity is up to your imagination, but in general, it can include heights to jump, tunnels to go through, or some sort of strip surface you can walk on.

A cone that moves from side to side is another easy option. Teach your dog to overcome each obstacle individually and gradually increase the difficulty until he manages to complete the course. You can do it yourself if you want.

Dogs That Dig

If you have a piece of land, even if it is small, you can give your dog an area where he can practice one of many people's favorite activities: digging. All they need is land.

Of course, when the dog goes outside, in addition to taking care that the environment is in order and avoiding water leaks, it is also necessary to provide a space with shade and fresh water at all times. By the way, if your dog is a water lover, then a bowl of water will be an excellent pastime.

Stimulates His Nose

You don't have many toys, and the dog is too small to see out the window, so how do you entertain your dog alone at home? Dogs love to smell everything, so hiding things somewhere in the house to entertain your furry friend before heading outside can stimulate their sense of smell. Let him find them. Remember, you must hide the treat somewhere where your dog can access it without getting hurt.

As you can see, how to keep him entertained when he is alone is a simpler task than it seems.

Planting

This game is one of the most used tricks to put a dog in a state of relaxation and well-being while training its sense of smell.

We are talking about foraging, or planting, a practice that consists of spreading some food or treats for dogs in outdoor spaces. Your pet will have a great time exploring the environment freely and in search of tasty treats. This game is also ideal for relaxing a dog suffering from stress or anxiety.

It is ideal if you have a patio at home where he can move quietly and rummage.

Puzzle

Dog puzzles are made of parts that cannot be swallowed or hurt. They consist of loose pieces that are just the right size, so they are not dangerous for your dog. These pieces hide candies that must be released in different ways. In some cases, candy will replace a piece. In other cases, the dog will have to move the pieces or even pick them up.

Ball Launcher

A ball launcher is ideal for the dog to play which you can also use indoors or outdoors. Your dog will have to pick up the ball, then he should throw it to the machine, and the machine will throw it back. Keep in mind that you should place the machine where the ball will not come out and break something.

Twister

Twister is one of the most popular games.

It's very exciting for high-IQ dogs.

The dogs have to move blocks to find treats. You can increase the difficulty by securing the blocks with pegs. The dog has to lift these pegs to move the blocks.

This very fun game provides a high level of mental stimulation.

Tornado

They are games that have rotating discs. The candies are hidden in compartments. Your dog has to rotate each level with his nose or paw in different directions to find them.

You can increase the difficulty by placing a bone-shaped white plastic block in one of the compartments.

You can also place treats under the white blocks, further increasing the difficulty.

You can make homemade models similar to the ones we prepared before.

Your Dog Shouldn't Last Long Alone

The amount of time a dog can stay in a home unaccompanied depends on several factors:

- Age: In general, puppies and adult dogs spend the least time alone at home due to their constant need for affection.
- State of health: A sick dog that needs medication cannot be alone for long, and loneliness will aggravate the state.

- Breed: Breeds that are more high-strung and anxious, like Chihuahuas, are more likely to be anxious when left alone than larger breeds, like German Shepherds.
- Emotional and behavioral issues: Dogs that have experienced trauma, such as being startled by the noise of a rocket when left alone, or a rude dog unable to control their impulses, need more supervision and attention.
- Canine personality: Self-sufficient dogs tend to be more determined and more independent, which helps them better tolerate time without others in the house.
- The time that the dog spends at home: In general, over time, the dog gets used to being at home and feels safe and confident, so it is not a problem to be alone for a few hours. As long as the waiting time is reasonable. However, new dogs can feel strange and intimidating, so being alone for too long can cause them more stress than usual.

The Bladder Is an Important Issue

Being home alone also means not going out, and your dog can't go out to relieve himself. To give you an idea of why it's important not to leave your dog alone for too long, consider that you're depriving him of "potty use."

Dogs usually need to be outside 3-5 times a day. These outings are more frequent for puppies, dogs with medical problems that require medication (such as kidney failure), or older dogs.

Here is more detailed information and suggested departure times according to the age of the dog:

- For puppies younger than 8 months, you can use the months of their lives as a guide for how long they can go without going outside. For example, one-month-old puppies should go out every hour, three-month-olds every three hours, and so on.

- Adult dogs must be outside at least every 8 hours.
- For dogs older than 10 years, the frequency of walks may vary depending on the state of health. They can usually wait 3-6 hours for short walks.

Take your dog's outdoor activities very seriously because if you force him to hold his urine for a long time, in addition to constant discomfort, he will be more prone to urinary infections.

Puppies are sensitive animals that need love and affection. Remember, they arrived at a new house without their mother and brothers not long ago.

Going from suddenly being in his den to being completely alone can negatively affect your dog's attitude. Therefore, the amount of time your pup spends alone should be kept to a minimum.

When your puppy first comes home, you shouldn't leave him unattended for more than 2 hours, and 4 in a very specific way where you have no choice.

If you enlist the help of family or neighbors to walk your pup every few hours, they'll be happy, and the effects of loneliness won't be as strong.

In case there is no one to help, there could be someone in charge of walking the dog in free time. Hire a trusted person, or, if it's a stranger, buy a security camera for the dog, and if that person fulfills his role, you can control him too.

Little by little, when he is about 6 months old and knows how to control the urge to go to the bathroom in the street, you can increase the waiting time to 6 hours.

Going back to the topic of games when you are alone, the puzzle game—which is one of the most recommended—is done because:

- Your dog will be happy with any puzzle that involves mental stimulation.
- There are different games for dogs of different sizes and intelligence levels.
- Your dog will be busy trying to get a treat.
- Using puzzles correctly can relax your dog and prevent destructive behavior.
- Beware of sweets and being overweight. When you are going to use it for a long time, limit its administration or replace them with their croquettes.
- Puzzles are not a substitute for the daily socialization or physical activity your dog should have.
- Dog puzzles do not solve separation anxiety or aggression problems.
- Consult an expert to solve these problems.
- Teach your dog to play his puzzles and participate in the game.
- Solving challenges with you will make your dog very happy. Reward your success with joy and congratulations.
- Monitor games and save them when you're done.
- Remember, no toy is indestructible. Remove it when it is defective or damaged.

CHAPTER 7

WHY VARIETY IN A DOG'S EXERCISE ROUTINE IS IMPORTANT

Exercise is just as important for dogs as it is for people. Regular exercise is known to provide mental health in addition to physical health.

Through physical activity, dogs can release tension and, together with a balanced diet, establish a healthy lifestyle. So why not provide your pet with this basic health requirement? In this chapter, we will talk about why it is important to ensure your dog gets aerobic exercise.

Exercise has been shown to reduce anxiety in dogs. All pet owners need to make sure their pups are in good shape; this simple measure can prevent you from coming home to find your sofa chewed up.

Lack of exercise and mental stimulation has been known to cause dogs to display destructive behavior to get your attention.

If He Stays Physically and Mentally Active, He Ages More Slowly

Of course, for dogs, just like humans, moderate exercise helps keep the mind sharp. This translates into a lower incidence of age-related diseases.

Of course, the exercise can be adapted to the life stage of your pet. Remember, while senior dogs need to stay active, excessive exercise will never do any good. Therefore, it is highly recommended that you seek your veterinarian's advice on the right amount and type of exercise for your dog.

You Help Him Prevent Mental Illnesses and Osteoarthritis

It's no secret that regular exercise is one of the best ways to keep your pet's joints healthy. Remember, it's not just about maintaining enough weight to avoid stress. This exercise also ensures that the joints remain lubricated while strengthening the supporting muscles.

There is no doubt that when dogs exercise with their owners, their emotional bonds are strengthened. Since exercise is such an exhilarating activity, sharing a workout can strengthen friendships. Even something as simple as a daily walk will improve your mental and cardiovascular balance.

Of course, you should always put yourself in the place of your pet. For example, when running on the beach, you should consider that shells can be painful for your dog's sensitive paws. Also, exercising in the sun for a few more hours could give your best friend heat stroke.

Dogs Need to Work

Remember, the person is choosing the dog to do a specific job. Your friend's ancestors were bred for hunting, herding, or other purposes. For this reason, your dog must be able to act on his instincts to some degree.

It's not about taking him on the hunt, it's about providing interesting opportunities to perform tasks according to his needs and breed. If a dog doesn't have a job for his breed and age, like chasing a frisbee, he assigns it to himself, like barking at passers-by or littering. Read about the type of dog you have to help you adjust.

Exercise in Dogs Leads to Obedience

Who is a good dog? The one who exercises. If you want your pup to obey you more happily, more interactive activities may be the key. When you spend time playing with your dog and teaching him new games, the bond is strengthened and leads to more submissive behavior.

Exercise Opens the Way for Better Socialization

Exercise can and should be part of a daily routine of exposure to other dogs, people, and environmental stimuli. This is a very effective way of putting a puppy on the path to proper socialization.

It's important to note that for most dogs, a leisurely walk around the block simply won't meet their aerobic exercise needs. However, lively playtime with other dogs at the park can promote their socialization and ensure puppies get an adequate level of exercise.

Let's Not Forget His Mental Health

The mental health of animals is largely forgotten, but it is just as important as physical health. For a domestic dog to be happy, its mind must be balanced in all aspects.

It's easy to forget about the mental health of pets. If it is often overlooked in humans, it is not uncommon for it to appear in non-humans, who also express themselves in other languages that we do not understand. Therefore, here you can read tips to take care of your dog's mental health, one of the most common animals in your home.

First, you will discover the general psychological profile of a canine, which is crucial in formulating his care. Later, you can read fun tips to improve his emotional and mental life, so do not miss them.

To take care of your dog's mental health, you must have a knowledge base that allows you to identify his needs, personality, and problems early. Dogs are complex creatures that have been around us for a long time, so we have the instinctual ability and cultural background to understand them.

However, here are some notes to organize the ideas to be presented in future lines:

- Dogs are hierarchical animals: The "have to know who is the boss" style has disappeared from dog behavior books, but dogs live in vertical organizations, so most need you for guidance, or they'll try what they are, and with that, trouble comes.
- They are gregarious: If they don't have enough healthy social interactions, they develop behavioral disorders. For example, a dog cannot be alone all day.
- They are carnivorous: Not all dogs have a well-developed hunting instinct, but this condition dictates part of their behavior. An example is the style of play. The rabbit plays tag and trains to escape, the dog plays with biting and fighting.
- Their behavior is usually stable: They are regular animals. Unexpected or strong changes in a dog's behavior are always warning signs.
- They are empathic: They are often able to recognize and be influenced by their emotional circumstances. To a greater or lesser extent, they will be able to know how you feel, and that is something that must be taken into account.

Of course, each dog has a way of being, and the needs that arise from his nature are only the basis for specific care. Next, I will leave you a series of tips so that you develop the necessary skills to take care of the mind of your canine companion.

In addition to what was seen before, I will show you some tips to take care of your dog's mental health.

Many of these tips may seem obvious to you, but sometimes it can be difficult to put them into practice if you're not paying attention. In either case, humility and an open mind are crucial in recognizing your dog's needs. Starting from this assumption will make it easier for you to carry out all the instructions that I want to show you.

Know Your Dog

If you don't know your dog as well as you know your human relatives, it can be hard to miss what he needs to be happy. Take the time to figure out what he likes, what he lacks, and what he does when he's sad or stressed. You don't have to be a behavioral expert, but you do need to know when something might be wrong in his mental life.

Learn a Lot

Information is the power to change mistakes. Read, research, and talk to experts. Being humble and putting yourself in the hands of professionals is not incompatible with having useful knowledge in the prevention and management of complications that arise when treating your dog.

Take Care of His Diet

The relationship between mental health and diet is not something that is perceived in a very obvious way, but it is there. A poor diet can cause health problems that can affect your dog's emotional or mental state, but there is also a direct relationship between a poor diet and mental health.

Enrich His Life

As with any animal, including humans, boredom is dangerous to a dog's mind in the long run. There are tons of ways to keep things fresh in their lives: games, training, candy, outings, toys, and more.

Plus, with so many options, a dog can maintain his independence and security while spending special time with you.

Have a Routine

Dogs require a routine in their daily lives. Breaking it up from time to time is normal, but an unstable and constantly changing environment can eventually create chronic anxiety and insecurity for them. Don't be afraid to always take them for a walk in the same place, give them the same food for long periods, or do activities always at the same time.

Calm Is Important for His Mental Health

As stated above, dogs are empathic animals, for example, they can comfort us when we're sad and cheer us up when we're happy. This quality is one of the things that most unites humans since it greatly facilitates coexistence and understanding.

For this reason, like any other social creature, living in an environment of tension or conflict can promote things like anxiety, depression, and aggression in dogs.

People have their ups and downs, and that's okay. In any case, every guardian must be aware that his emotional state is transmitted to the dog since the feelings of the owner can also affect his emotional well-being.

The last tip is foresighted: If you don't feel capable or you haven't welcomed a dog into your home at the right time, you better not do it. Plus, it's easy to see claims that living with dogs can improve human mental health.

CHAPTER 8

BONUS: FUN AND CHALLENGING EXERCISE PROGRAM FOR YOUR DOG

The next time your dog looks at you with droopy eyes, consider this: Your friend could be downright bored. For an intelligent dog—as your furry friend surely is—taking a walk around the block is not enough to motivate them during the day. In other words, this will be as if you asked Einstein at school, "How much is one plus one?"

These exercises will help you to strengthen yourself and improve how your dog communicates with you and exercises his mind.

The Pot Game

For this one, you need a pot and sweets and patience to prepare it.

How to Do It

1. Give your dog a treat (a simple pellet of feed is not worth it, use something irresistible) and an empty plastic container. Put the treat on the ground, let your dog eat it, and lick its lips. Now, place another treat on the ground, but cover it lightly with the pan so your friend can easily pick it up.
2. Place the treat on the ground and cover it with the pot, so your

friend has to push it to get to his food. Add more pots as you master the game. The dog's challenge gets tricky: your friend has to guess which jar the prize is under.

3. Tip: Don't make it so hard that your pup can't find it. Take it little by little: it's about putting your mind to work, but above all, having fun.

The Hidden Cheese: Find It

Another great game to start with is the smell game that your dog loves. For this, make him win a prize: slices of cheese or sausage, for example.

How to Do It

1. First, get one slice of cheese or sausage for your furry friend.
2. Next, throw him at your feet and give him the command: "Find him!" Easy right? Let's complicate things: once he's gobbled up the treat, he'll look at you. Throw it a little further and say: "Look for it!"

- Tip 1: Keep playtime short at first and you will always be successful with your dog. Once your dog has mastered the game, you can complicate the game and hide the cheese parts.
- Tip 2: Drop the next piece only when it comes back to you. This is how you learn another important lesson for your partner: come when you call.

Following Clues

Those who live with dogs are in no doubt about it, but science has proven it: Our furry companions are experts at deciphering the art of our body posture. Do not miss this mastery of the puppy that activates his brain: you can teach him to run to the right, run to the left, lie down, sit, or come when you call him.

How to Do It

1. It is very important to keep your dog calm before you start. If he is very excited, it is best to play with him first and then take him out for a walk to calm him down. Once he's calm, it's time to start.
2. Strong-smelling food is the perfect bait to attract your dog's attention and also leave an easy-to-follow trail. Canned wet foods are a good place to start.
3. Have a friend hold your dog and start preparing the area while he can't see you. This step is important because if he's looking at where you put food, he may not be using his senses, which are crucial to advancing the quest.
4. Rub some food on the grass to make a path, use the food to carve a path, and leave a piece at the end of the path for snacks. That way, your dog will think that searching is always worth it.
5. Once the path is prepared, have your dog on a leash and encourage him to search. Use explicit commands like "fetch" to get your dog used to the command.
6. If he doesn't seem to be in the way, help him out and point to the area with your finger. Keep repeating the word "fetch" throughout.
7. In the end, your dog will find the way and reach the final prize, and we will let him rest once the practice is over.

Walks and Active Nose

This game is the easiest to play but perhaps the most important. When you go for a walk, remember that your dog lives in a world full of smells: his nose has about 220 million receptor cells (some dogs have even more)—many times the number that our noses contain ten times. So instead of turning your friend into a robot on a leash, let him smell as he walks.

If he's happy, don't be disappointed: he's just a dog. Instead, take this opportunity to teach him a new trick. In this case, the pattern "sniffs": you can use it to reward your friend when he sniffs calmly without pulling on the leash and stops to get it right. When you think he's ready, use the "OK, let's go" pattern, reward him, and move on.

Plus, sniff walks are great for older or less mobile dogs who don't walk long distances—you can get your pal out of the house to give him a mental boost without having to run a marathon. Go with him to a fun place your friend likes, like a nature walk or a walk on the beach, or you can go for a snack at a dog-friendly place where your friend is welcome.

Stacking Rings

Just like with the toys made before or how we teach children to have hand and eye control, you can also teach dogs eye-paw or mouth-eye coordination. One of my favorite games is this one.

This is a difficult game that takes a while to learn, so you and your dog will have to work together for hours as it takes days or even weeks to perfect the game. It is important to find wooden rings with natural stains and not plastic, as your dog will chew everything and can crush them. The size you need to buy depends on the size and agility of your dog's mouth.

Clicker training is ideal for this because your dog feels rather than sees what it is doing.

How to Do It

1. Click first and treat your dog when he hears the click.
2. Then click and treat as you move the edge closer to the stick where the rim will enter.
3. Continue creating, clicking, and hitting it while touching the ring with the stick, then try placing the ring on top of the stick.

It is a game of patience so that the dog learns to fit the rings on the stick of the toy. You can show him, using command words or the clicker, so that he knows what he will do every time he hears it.

Hot and Cold

The hot and cold game is also great for clicker training because it follows the basics to shape new behaviors. It's perfect for a smart dog who doesn't get frustrated too easily. All you have to do is sit on the couch and say "hot" or "cold" and have something to earn. It sounds easy, right?

How to Do It

1. Basically, all you have to do is figure out what you want your dog to do. It could be anything, maybe you see your keys on the ground and want your dog to pick them up and bring them back.
2. Just step back with your treat bag, and every time the dog

moves into that area, you enthusiastically say "hot" and toss the treat right where it is. If your dog strays from his chosen target, you calmly say, "cold." If it moves towards the chosen target, you say "Hot!" with enthusiasm and treat it.

You could have your dog touch a doorknob across the room, grab a blanket off the couch, or pretty much any behavior you can think of. The idea of making movements and learning with what was explained before.

Jump Rope

Eye and body coordination is combined in this game. Your dog has to focus on the rhythm of the rope, the orientation to a particular point on the ground, and of course, the jump.

How to Do It

1. Start by teaching your dog to orient himself using objects on the ground. For example, you can use a stick that not only tells the dog where to jump but also how much room there is to keep the dog's sides within range of the rope.
2. Once you find it, teach your dog to use the cue to jump to that spot.
3. Once this is done, add the rope and put your foot on top of your dog each time he needs to jump when the rope goes down.
4. This trick takes a lot of practice, but it also uses a lot of extra energy from your dog's brain and body.

CONCLUSIONS

It can be difficult to control claustrophobia in the winter or when we must be at home and our dog too, especially for active dogs who like to get out and play. Being stuck indoors can lead to boredom. But you can keep your dog entertained with some puzzles and activities just like the ones we saw in this book.

With just a few supplies, each DIY activity comes together easily and will give your furry the entertainment they've been craving.

Puzzle games are puzzle pieces, toys, and activities that encourage your dog to experiment and solve problems. They are great for dogs with high energy levels, especially anxious or high-energy dogs.

Puzzle games should be used under direct supervision to avoid ingestion of any materials used to make the toy.

Everyone loves a game of fetch with their dog. It's great for exercising and having fun. But the disadvantage of the game is that they don't have to think, they just have to run from one side to another. So many games with dogs—from fetch to tug-of-war—don't require much thought.

On the other hand, interactive puzzle games tire out an energetic dog, beat boredom, boost self-confidence, and strengthen the bond between the two of you while working as a team. Many great activities you can do with your dog are just canine versions of children's favorite games, all of which exercise and train the brain and body.

Letting your dog use his nose to find hidden treasures is a great way to stimulate his brain and teach him to use all of his senses. First of all, you need to set your dog up for success so that he understands the game and doesn't get too discouraged. Start with simple things. Sit your dog down, hide his favorite treats or toys in plain sight, and even let your dog watch you while you hide them. Then give your dog the release signal to get the toy. Reward your dog for successfully finding hidden treasure.

Increase the excitement and reward levels of the popular treasure hunt game by becoming the treasure your dog is in charge of finding. You need at least two people to play. One distracts the dog and tells it to sit while the other hides. The person with the dog gives the release signal, allowing the dogs to begin searching. Great both indoors and out, this game is a fun way to play with your dog on a rainy afternoon.

In short, you have many options to prepare with your pet. The plan is that you use, in the homemade ones, materials that, if eaten, do not harm the dog and try to make the toys so well that they do not break easily, adapting them to the type of dog, size, and physical condition.

Remember, developing these skills takes time; the journey is part of the game, so be patient. It may take quite a few sessions before your dog understands what "put it away" means. But watching your dog learn and solve problems is part of the fun. When your dog is feeling down, silence or just a little encouragement can build confidence while helping him find the skill.

If you made it this far, I highly value your reading and would appreciate a positive review and comment so that other people can benefit from the book.

Thank you, and good luck with your pet!

Made in the USA
Las Vegas, NV
27 July 2023